SEAHORSE CONNECTIONS

HELPING MY CHILD

A Guide to Supporting Reading

GRADE
3

SEAHORSE
PUBLISHING

TABLE OF CONTENTS

THE SCIENCE OF READING

Reading is an essential skill for success in school and in life. In order to understand how children learn to read, parents should understand the science of reading.

The *science of reading* is a term that refers to more than 20 years of research by experts on how people learn to read. The research shows that reading does not come naturally. For many people, it takes significant effort. Learning how to read is most effective when it happens in a step-by-step process that is based on proven, research-supported strategies and techniques.

Good reading instruction has several important parts. It helps students develop skills in phonological awareness, phonics, fluency, vocabulary, and comprehension. All these skills help students build pathways in their brains that connect speech sounds to print and that connect words with their meanings. By using the science of reading as a guide, parents and teachers can support our children in learning how to read.

KEYS TO EFFECTIVE READING INSTRUCTION

Phonological Awareness: The ability to notice, think about, and work with the sounds that make up spoken words

Phonics: Understanding the relationship between sounds and the letters that represent them in written words

Fluency: The ability to read quickly and accurately

Vocabulary: Understanding word meanings

Comprehension: Gaining meaning from reading

CREATING SKILLED READERS

Reading is more than just sounding out words. Skilled readers are able to recognize words as well as understand their meanings on a deep level. They weave together memorization skills, phonics skills, vocabulary skills, background knowledge, and more.

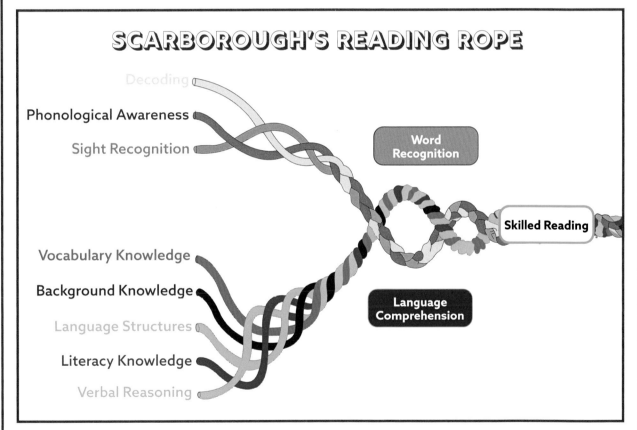

To show how children draw on a variety of abilities to become skilled readers, Dr. Hollis Scarborough created the Reading Rope. In 2001, this model was published in the *Handbook of Early Literacy Research* (Neuman/Dickinson).

PHONOLOGICAL AND PHONEMIC AWARENESS:
HEARING SOUNDS IN WORDS

Phonological awareness and phonemic awareness are important pre-reading skills. They describe a child's ability to hear, identify, and play with sounds in spoken language. These skills form an essential foundation for reading and writing development in third grade and beyond.

Children demonstrate phonological awareness when they recognize and manipulate, or change, parts of spoken words. Phonemic awareness is the last phonological awareness skill to develop. Children who have mastered phonemic awareness can hear, recognize, and play with the individual sounds, or phonemes, in spoken words.

PHONOLOGICAL AWARENESS MILESTONES

Ages 3 to 4	Produces real and pretend rhyming words
Ages 4 to 5	Claps or taps out syllables in words Recognizes words that begin with the same sound Segments or separates out each sound in words with three sounds Blends or combines individual sounds to produce words that have three sounds Counts the number of sounds in words that have three sounds
Ages 5 to 6	Segments or separates out each sound in words with four sounds Identifies the first and last sounds in a word Groups words with the same beginning sound Identifies which word does not rhyme in a set of three words Identifies which word is not the same in a set of three words
Ages 6 to 7	Deletes syllables from words when asked Deletes sounds from words when asked Substitutes syllables in words when asked Substitutes sounds in words when asked
Ages 7 to 8	Uses phonological awareness skills to spell words

ACTIVITIES FOR BUILDING PHONOLOGICAL AWARENESS

SYLLABLE HUNT
Look around the house to find things whose names have more than one syllable. Say the word and hold up a finger for each word part. For example, say, "bed-room" for bedroom and "ma-ca-ro-ni" for macaroni.

SWITCH IT

Think of a one-syllable word. Ask your child to change the beginning, middle, or ending sound in the word to make a new word. Use this example, reading letters shown in between slash marks as sounds.

Parent: Change the /st/ sound in *stop* to /sh/. What is the new word?

Child: Shop.

Parent: Great job! Now, change the /ō/ sound in *float* to /ă/. What is the new word?

Child: Flat.

Parent: Excellent thinking. Try changing the /nk/ sound in *sink* to /ng/. What is the new word?

Child: Sing.

Parent: Terrific! You did it!

WORD MAGIC GAME

The adult says a word. The child changes the beginning, middle, or ending sound to make a new word and says what changed. The adult changes the beginning, middle, or ending sound of the child's word to make a new word and says what changed. Keep going back and forth. How far can you go? Use this example, reading letters shown between slash marks as sounds.

Parent: Mop.

Child: Top. I changed /m/ to /t/.

Parent: Stop. I changed /t/ to /st/.

Child: Step. I changed /ŏ/ to /ĕ/.

Parent: Stem. I changed /p/ to /m/.

Child: Them. I changed /st/ to /th/.

Parent: Hmm. I can't think of a change that makes a real word. You win!

PHONICS:
LETTERS
MAKE
SOUNDS

Phonics is the knowledge that letters and combinations of letters represent sounds. This is an essential skill for beginning readers. Children who have the benefit of phonics instruction become better readers and spellers.

All words are made up of sounds. The word *dog* has three sounds. Each letter stands for one sound. The word *light* has three sounds. The letters *igh* represent one sound. The English language uses 44 sounds to make all words. However, there are only 26 letters in the alphabet. Some letters can make more than one sound. Other letters combine to make new sounds. This is like a code that beginning readers must figure out.

PHONICS BENEFITS
- Improved reading ability
- Faster ability to match sounds to letters
- Easier time sounding out unknown words
- Reading level increases faster

PHONICS 101
KEEP IT SHORT
To avoid confusing beginning readers, don't add a vowel sound when you make consonant sounds. For example, the sound for letter *t* is /t/, not /tuh/.

ACTIVITIES
FOR BUILDING
PHONICS SKILLS

SHAVING CREAM LETTERS
Squirt shaving cream onto a large baking sheet. Spread it around evenly. Choose a letter or group of letters that makes a single sound. Say the sound. Use a finger to write the letter in the shaving cream and say its name. Say the sound the letter makes as you underline it. You can also do this with whipped cream!

CONSONANTS

Consonant letters are *b, c, d, f, g, h, j, k, l, m, n, p, q, r, s, t, v, w, x, y* (as in *you*), and *z*.

VOWELS: SHORT OR LONG?

Vowel letters are *a, e, i, o, u,* and *y* (as in *my* and *baby*). Short vowels are marked with a curved symbol, like a smile on top: /ă/. Long vowels are marked with a horizontal line on top: /ā/.

RAINBOW LETTERS

Draw a set of rainbow arches with space in between. Under the rainbow, write a letter or group of letters that makes one sound. Then, begin with the top arch. Use a red marker or crayon.

Follow these steps:

1. Say the sound the letter or letters make.

2. Write the letter or letters and say their names as you write.

3. Underline the letter or group of letters and say the sound it makes.

Repeat until the first arch is filled. Then, use an orange marker or crayon to fill the second arch in the same way as you say, write and spell, underline and read. Repeat for the next arches using different colors.

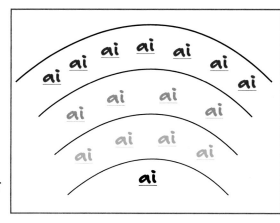

Sound Sort

On individual index cards, write letters or groups of letters that make one sound. Sort them into groups such as long a sound, long e sound, long i sound, long o sound, long u sound, or special vowel sound. Are there other ways to categorize the cards?

DECODING:
SOUNDS MAKE WORDS

Decoding is the ability to sound out written words. Children use their knowledge of the phonics code to figure out words. A child with strong word decoding skills will have better reading comprehension skills.

When your child can see a word, understand the sound each letter represents, and blend sounds together to say the word, they are decoding. Once they can decode words independently, they have the tools they need to begin reading with fluency and comprehension.

SOUNDING OUT WORDS

Segmentation means breaking a word into its individual sounds.
> **dog:** /d/ /ŏ/ /g/   **sheep:** /sh/ /ē/ /p/

Blending means putting the sounds in a word together without pauses. Try these techniques to help your child with blending.

Continuous Blending: Stretch out each sound so that it continues into the next. Use your finger to slide across each letter from left to right.
slip: sssssllllllllliiiiiiiip

Final Blending: Blend the first sounds together and then add the final sound.
slip: sli-p

Isolated Blending: Say the first sound the loudest and then say each following sound softer. The last sound will be the softest.
slip: S l i p

ACTIVITIES FOR BUILDING DECODING SKILLS

HIGHLIGHT IT
Use two different colors to highlight the consonant letters and vowel letters in a list of words.

green   **think**

MARK IT
In a list of words, mark vowel letters *v* and consonant letters *c*. Underline any letters that go together (vowel teams, consonant blends, consonant teams, etc.).

gr ee n   th i nk
c c v v c   c c v c c

BOX IT
In a list of words, draw boxes around letters that go together.

gr ee n   th i nk

SIGHT WORDS AND HIGH-FREQUENCY WORDS:
BUILDING BLOCKS FOR SUCCESS

Knowing sight words and high-frequency words helps create a strong foundation for beginning readers. Both types of words are often used in reading and writing. A sight word is a word that does not follow the regular rules of phonics and spelling. It is not decodable or is very difficult to decode. High-frequency words are decodable words that students need to know in order to be fluent readers. However, the phonics rules needed to decode them might not have been taught yet.

The word *like* is a high-frequency word. It can be decoded using the "magic *e*" or "bossy *e*" rule. Children who are just learning to read words such as *cat* and *sit* have not been taught this rule. However, since *like* is used in many simple stories, it is often introduced as a high-frequency word.

The word *have* is a sight word. It occurs often, but it does not follow the "magic *e*" or "bossy *e*" rule. Therefore, this word must be memorized, or identified by sight.

GETTING UNSTUCK

What to do when your child gets stuck reading a word, or when they decode a word incorrectly? Allow time for your child to figure it out. Gently offer these strategies.

- Spell the word.
- Ask, "Do you see any letters that go together?"
- Ask, "Do you see any little words inside the longer word?"
- Say, "Let's sound out each part."

SMALL BUT MIGHTY

Just 13 words make up 25 percent of all English words in print.

a	of
and	that
for	the
he	to
in	was
is	you
it	

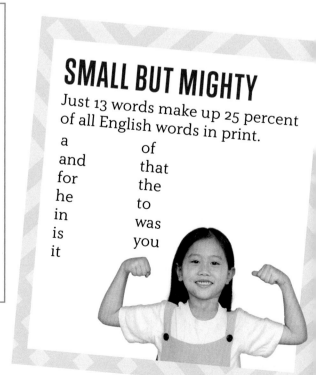

ACTIVITIES FOR LEARNING SIGHT WORDS AND HIGH-FREQUENCY WORDS

Slap It!

Choose five words to learn. Write each on a sticky note. Place the notes around the house. When your child finds a word, have them read the word and then use their hand to slap it.

COLORFUL WORDS

Write a word in the middle of a sheet of paper. Have your child choose a colored marker or pencil. Read the word. Have your child write the word in color, saying the name of each letter aloud as it is written. Underline the word from left to right while reading the word. Then, choose a new color and repeat. Keep choosing new colors until you have filled the page.

Trace It

Write words on index cards. Have your child read each word aloud. Ask your child to use their index finger to trace each letter while saying its name. Then, use a finger to underline the word from left to right while reading the word. Repeat with the next card.

WORD ATTACK SKILLS:
WORDS HAVE PARTS

Skilled readers can look at unfamiliar words and chunk them, or break them into smaller parts. This helps them attack words and figure out how to read them and what they mean. When readers use chunking, they are sometimes looking at the letters in words. Sometimes, they are looking at the syllables that make up words. Other times, they are looking at prefixes, suffixes, and other word parts. Typically, skilled readers are doing all three. Knowing how to break down words is important for growing as a reader and developing fluency. Third graders encounter an increasing number of longer words in their school day. Having good word attack skills is essential.

TYPES OF SYLLABLES

CLOSED	OPEN	MAGIC E	VOWEL TEAM	R-CONTROLLED	CONSONANT + LE
hat rab-bit	me ba-by	time rep-tile	coat rac-coon	farm mar-ket	cas-tle ap-ple
Consonant is after the vowel.	Vowel is at the end of the syllable.	Has the vowel-consonant-silent e pattern.	Has two or more vowel letters together.	Vowel is followed by the letter r.	Has consonant and le at the end of a word.
short vowel sound	long vowel sound	long vowel sound	long, short, or special sound	/ar/, /or/, /ur/	consonant + /l/ sound

BREAKING DOWN A WORD

Compound Word: Is it made of two smaller words? Draw a line between them.

Suffix (Ending): Does it end in -ed, -ing, -ful, -tion, etc.? Draw a line before the suffix.

Prefix (Beginning): Does it begin with pre-, un-, dis-, etc.? Draw a line after the prefix.

Double Letters: Do double consonants come between two vowels? Draw a line between the double consonants.

V-C-C-V: Are there two consonants (that don't make one sound together) between two vowels? Draw a line between the two consonants.

V-C-V: Is there one consonant between two vowels? Or a consonant team between two vowels?

-Try drawing a line after the first vowel. That makes the first syllable open and the vowel long. Is that a word? If not, try the first vowel as short e. Is that a word?

-Try drawing a line after the consonant or consonant team. That makes the first syllable closed and the vowel short. Is that a word?

ACTIVITIES FOR BUILDING WORD ATTACK SKILLS

CHALLENGE

Get a list of two-, three-, and four-syllable words. Use a timer to see who is the fastest at using their syllable, chunking, and phonics skills to read the words.

Make the Word

Get a list of two-syllable words. Write each syllable on a separate index card. Each word will have one card for the first syllable and one card for the second syllable. Mix up all the cards and place them facedown. The first player flips over two cards. If they make a word, the player keeps the cards and goes again. If the cards do not make a word, the player flips them back over and the next player tries to make a match. Keep going until all cards have a match. The person with the most words wins.

SYLLABLE HUNT

Choose one type of syllable (for example, closed syllables) or one strategy for breaking down a word (for example, dividing between double consonants). Search in books for words that have that type of syllable or that work with that dividing strategy. Write them in a list. How many can you find?

VIDEO TEACHER

Work with your child to create a short video that teaches others how to use the syllable rules to break large words into parts. With your child's approval, share it with your child's teacher.

FLUENCY: READING WITH EASE

Fluency is the ability to read with reasonable speed and expression. A fluent reader doesn't have to stop to decode each word. They can focus on what the story or text means. Fluency is the bridge between decoding words and comprehension.

Your third grader is reading smoothly. When they read aloud, their tone and expression change to match the meaning of the text and to respond to what is happening in the story. Most third graders begin the school year reading about 80 to 90 words per minute. The goal is to read 120 words per minute by the end of the year. The best way to increase this speed is to practice, practice, practice.

RECORD IT

After your child practices reading a book, make an audio or video recording of them reading the book aloud. Play it back. Discuss what went well and what to improve on. If your child desires, record again.

FINDING BOOKS THAT ARE JUST RIGHT

ACTIVITIES FOR BUILDING FLUENCY

BOOK OF THE WEEK CHALLENGE

Choose a book that has about 75 to 100 words. It is okay if the words or sentences repeat. On Sunday, read the book together at least once. Set a timer and have your child read it aloud. Record the time it takes your child to read. Note if your child needed help. Read the same book on Monday. Time your child again and note if help was needed. Continue the process every day for a week. At the end, show your child the evidence of how they are improving in fluency.

TRACK IT

Select a one-page passage or a chapter book page. Use the "Just Right" guidelines below to make sure the reading level of the page is right for your child. Create a fluency tracker chart like the one shown at right. Label it with the name of the reading selection. Set a timer for 60 seconds. Have your child begin reading. Remind them to focus on reading with expression, not just on speed. When the timer goes off, mark the fluency tracker. At the bottom of one column, note the date and the number of words read correctly in one minute. Shade the column to show how many words were read. Use a different color for each day your child practices.

Name: _Mateo_   **Title:** _The BFG, page 20_

Fluency Tracker

	1/17	1/19						
130								
120								
110								
100								
90								
80								
70		▓						
60		▓						
50	░	▓						
40	░	▓						
30	░	▓						
20	░	▓						
10	░	▓						
Date/WPM	1/17 50	1/19 65						

TOO EASY

You know all the words.

You can easily retell the story.

You have read the book many times before.

You are reading too fast.

Does this describe your book? Try a more difficult book.

JUST RIGHT

- You know most of the words.
- You understand what you are reading, and you can retell it.
- You are reading at a steady pace.

Does this describe your book? This book is just right for you!

TOO HARD

- There are lots of tricky words.
- You forget important information as you read.
- You are reading too slowly.

Does this describe your book? Try an easier book.

VOCABULARY:
WORDS HAVE MEANING

Vocabulary plays a critical role in the process of learning to read. Young readers use their knowledge about words to make sense of what they are reading. In order to understand what is read, a child must know what the words mean. Children need a large mental "word bank" to draw on as they read. The larger a child's vocabulary, the more they are able to comprehend what they are reading or listening to.

As new words are encountered, children link them to words they already know to add to their growing vocabularies. Some words are learned naturally. Others must be taught. Children learn new words through daily conversations and by having experiences that teach them about the world. Reading books to your child also exposes them to rich language.

MAP IT!

Create a thinking map. Write a vocabulary word in the center of a sheet of paper. Then, divide the paper into four sections. In the first box, write a simple definition. In the second box, write examples or words that mean the same as the vocabulary word. In the third box, make a connection to something in your life or something you know. In the fourth box, add a picture that represents the word.

Definition	Examples/Synonyms
to get the same kinds of things and keep them	gather save

collect

Connection	Picture
I collect stuffies.	

TYPES OF VOCABULARY

Listening Vocabulary: The words we hear
Speaking Vocabulary: The words we say
Reading Vocabulary: The words we read
Writing Vocabulary: The words we use to write

ACTIVITIES FOR BUILDING VOCABULARY

WORDS FROM NONFICTION

Choose a nonfiction book. Read the book aloud with your child. Talk about new words from the book. Have your child share with others the new words they learned.

NEW WORD TALK

Introduce a new word to your child by providing a simple definition. Then, give an example that relates to your child's experiences. Have your child think of an example, too. Over the next few days, take the opportunity to use the new word in conversation.

NEW WORDS WHILE READING

When your child is reading, it is okay to stop to discuss a new word. Reread the sentence and ask what your child thinks the new word means. Give a child-friendly definition. Help your child make a personal connection to the word.

MY VOCABULARY JOURNAL

Have your child keep a vocabulary journal. Use a spiral-bound notebook or composition book. Write one vocabulary word on each page. Draw a picture that represents the word. Write a kid-friendly definition. Write a sentence that uses the word.

COMPREHENSION:
UNDERSTANDING
WHAT IS READ

Reading comprehension is the essence of reading. It is the ability to gain meaning from what you read. This is a complex skill that develops over time. Children can begin growing in this area by taking time to think about what they have just read. As children read, their minds must be "turned on" and thinking actively about what they are reading.

Third graders should be able to understand books they read and books that are read to them. They can answer questions about a story. They can find evidence by looking through the book. For fiction books, they can tell about the characters, setting, and important events. For nonfiction books, they can give important facts from the book by stating who, what, when, where, and why.

LOL!	Funny part
*	Important part
!	Surprising or shocking part
?	Confusing part or unknown word
—✗—	Part where I made a connection
👁	Part where I visualized something
💭	Part where I predicted something
🔍	Part where I understood something

ACTIVE READING

Active reading happens when the reader is involved and engaged with the text. The reader is thinking about what is being read and making connections. This type of reading is essential for comprehension.

Help your child practice active reading by drawing symbols on sticky notes to show their thinking as they read. Use the examples above.

ACTIVITIES FOR BUILDING READING COMPREHENSION

SHARED READING

Choose a book. Read aloud the first paragraph or first couple of sentences. Talk about what was read. Have your child read the next paragraph or couple of sentences. Continue to discuss the story as you share the reading.

MAKE A NOTE (NONFICTION BOOKS)

Fold a sheet of paper into fourths. In the center of the paper, write the main topic of the book. Then, in each section, write a fact from the book. Draw pictures to go with the facts.

BEGINNING-MIDDLE-END (FICTION BOOKS)

Fold a sheet of paper into thirds. In the first section, draw and label a picture of what happened in the beginning of the story. In the second section, draw and label a picture of what happened in the middle. In the third section, draw and label a picture of what happened at the end of the story. Use the drawings to talk about and retell the story.

COMPREHENSION QUESTIONS

For Nonfiction (Real-World) Books

Before Reading
- What is the title? What clues does the title give about the book?
- What do you think you will learn by reading this book?

During Reading
- What questions do you have?
- How do the pictures and captions help you understand the words?

After Reading
- What is the book mainly about? Why is this topic important?
- What did you learn?
- How did the author make it easy to find information (through headings, charts, etc.)?

For Fiction Books

Before Reading
- Who is the author? Who is the illustrator? What do they do?
- What do you think will happen in the story?

During Reading
- What do you think will happen next? How do you think the character will react?
- Why do you think the character did that or said that?

After Reading
- What was the problem in the story? How was the problem solved?
- Is there a moral or lesson in this story?
- How does the main character change from the beginning to the end?

WRITING: SHOWING UNDERSTANDING

Children are often asked to write about what they read. They also write about their own ideas. When children write, they show their understanding of phonics, high-frequency words, vocabulary, and more. They demonstrate that they have internalized what they have learned and made it their own.

Third grade students are writing to express their ideas in more sophisticated ways. Their sentences are longer and more meaningful. Spelling is more accurate. Punctuation is used appropriately. There is correct subject-verb agreement.

WHEN WRITING IS HARD

- Use a text-to-speech feature on a computer. Then, have your child copy on paper.

- Use a thinking map. Write the topic in a box at the top of a sheet of paper. Underneath, draw three smaller boxes. Write or draw one detail or example in each small box. Use the map to help write a paragraph.

- Have your child tell you what to write. Help them create the sentences. When you are finished, your child can copy what you wrote.

- When your child starts writing, set a timer for 10 minutes. When the timer goes off, take a 10-minute break. Continue this pattern until the writing is complete.

ACTIVITIES FOR BUILDING WRITING SKILLS

POPPING WORDS

Good, big, nice. Some words are generic and don't make writing come alive. In a journal, write a generic word at the top of a page. Below, write more descriptive words that could replace it. As you find more words that add "pop" to your writing, add them to the journal. Use these examples.

good: *excellent, delightful, amazing*

big: *huge, gigantic, enormous*

nice: *kind, thoughtful, gracious*

COMBINE SENTENCES

Encourage your child to write longer, more complex sentences by combining two shorter sentences. Make it a game. Give each other pairs of short sentences to put together into one longer sentence. Can even more information be added to each longer sentence? Use these examples.

The corn was tasty.
The beans were tasty.
The corn and beans were tasty.

It was a nice day.
We had a picnic.
It was a nice day, so we had a picnic.

KEEP A JOURNAL

Encourage your child to keep a writing journal. It can include diary entries, questions, drawings, ideas, and lists. Occasionally, provide prompts for journal entries. For example, say, "write about what you would like to do this summer" or "write something you wonder about."

EDITING CHECKLIST

Read aloud. Does it make sense?

✔ Are there any words missing?

✔ Do all subjects and verbs agree?

✔ Is punctuation used correctly in each sentence?

✔ Are capital letters used at the beginning of sentences and proper names?

✔ Are all words spelled correctly?

WRITING:
HAVING A PURPOSE

Third graders write for a variety of purposes. They write to tell stories about personal experiences and the experiences of fictional characters. They write reports, articles, and presentations to explain information and facts. They write letters that persuade others to agree with their opinions. Writers at this age are learning to think about who will read what they write and how to make sure that their writing speaks to their specific audience.

In third grade, students can write a simple essay that includes a statement of the topic or main idea, examples or details that support the main idea, and a concluding sentence. They continue to build skills in researching, planning, organizing, revising, and editing with help. They use rubrics to score their writing and to understand what they need to improve.

TYPES OF WRITING

Narrative Writing: Tells a story

Informative Writing: Gives information

Opinion Writing: Gives an opinion

HOW TO WRITE A PARAGRAPH

A paragraph that gives information or expresses an opinion can be written with five sentences. The first sentence is the main idea or topic sentence that tells what the paragraph is going to explain. The next three sentences contain details or examples that support, prove, or explain the main idea. The fifth and last sentence closes up or ends the paragraph. Children can use the fingers on their hands to remind them of the parts needed for a good paragraph.

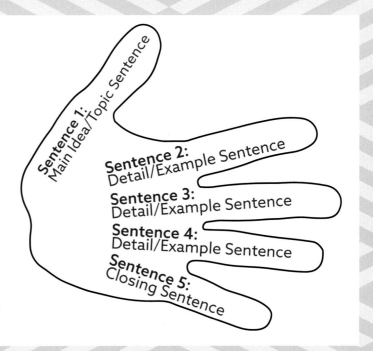

Sentence 1: Main Idea/Topic Sentence

Sentence 2: Detail/Example Sentence

Sentence 3: Detail/Example Sentence

Sentence 4: Detail/Example Sentence

Sentence 5: Closing Sentence

ACTIVITIES FOR BUILDING WRITING SKILLS

DETAILS, PLEASE

Choose a nonfiction book. Write the book's topic in the center of a sheet of paper and circle it. As your child reads, they can write details inside more circles that surround the center circle. Draw a line to connect each detail circle to the topic circle. Once there are at least four details, write a paragraph about the topic.

FAMILY STORIES

Encourage your child to learn your family's history by talking to you and to other relatives about stories from the past. What sport did Grandpa play when he was young? What happened to Aunt Rose on a camping trip? Your child can listen to lots of stories and then choose a favorite to write and illustrate. Publish the story by sharing it with family members.

INFORMATIVE/OPINION WRITING RUBRIC

Help your child use a rubric to understand expectations for their writing. Read and review this sample rubric with your child.

Standard	1 Needs Support	2 Approaching Standard	3 Meets Standard	4 Exceeds Standard
Introduces a topic. Groups related information together.	Does not introduce a topic or group related information.	Attempts to introduce a topic and to group related information.	Introduces a topic and groups related information.	Provides a strong introduction to a topic and groups related information.
Develops the topic with facts and details.	Does not develop the topic with facts and details.	Attempts to develop the topic with facts and details.	Develops the topic with facts and details.	Develops the topic with many facts and details.
Provides a concluding statement or section.	Does not provide a concluding statement or section.	Attempts to provide a concluding statement or section.	Provides a concluding statement or section.	Provides a strong concluding statement or section.
Shows command of capitalization, punctuation, and spelling.	Does not show a command of capitalization, punctuation, and spelling.	Attempts to show a command of capitalization, punctuation, and spelling.	Shows a command of capitalization, punctuation, and spelling.	Shows a strong command of capitalization, punctuation, and spelling.

SPELLING:
USING THE CODE

When children sound out a word, they use their knowledge of the phonics code to decode it. By contrast, when they spell a word, they use their knowledge of the phonics code to encode it. They must match a letter or group of letters to each sound heard in a word. Children can usually read words before they can spell them. But practicing spelling improves reading ability. Good spellers are generally good readers, and vice versa.

In third grade, students practice spelling words that follow phonics rules. They also spell frequently used words that don't follow phonics rules. Third graders are learning to spell many two-syllable words, including words with double consonants such as *happy* and *rabbit.* Common homophones, such as *there* and *their,* are also part of weekly spelling lists.

LEARNING TO SPELL RULE-BREAKERS

Many English words do not follow phonics rules. But it is still important for children to know how to spell them. Try these strategies.

Say, Spell and Write, Read and Underline: Say the word. Write the word while saying the name of each letter. Underline the word from left to right as you read it. Repeat five times in a row.

Triangle Word: Say the word. Write the first letter. Say the word. Write the first two letters. Say the word. Write the first three letters. Continue the pattern until the word is written. Then, say the word and write the full word three more times. See the example at right.

```
d
do
doe
does
does
does
does
```

Trace It: Write the word and read it. Trace each letter with your finger as you say its name. Use your finger to swipe under the word from left to right as you read it. Repeat three times. Then, close your eyes and use your finger to write each letter of the word in the air.

Chunk It: Break a longer word into syllables or groups of letters. Say the word. Write each chunk, saying the names of the letters as you write them. Pause after each chunk. Read the word. Repeat three times.

second: sec-ond   OR   se-co-nd

ACTIVITIES FOR BUILDING SPELLING SKILLS

SPOT IT

Write two lists of words side-by-side so that each word pair shows a word spelled correctly and incorrectly. Have your child find the correctly spelled words.

HOMOPHONE TRICKS

Some words sound the same, but have different meanings and spellings. Use the tricks below to remember the differences between homophones. Create your own tricks, too.

here and *hear*: I use my <u>ear</u> to h<u>ear</u>.

to and *too*: There are t<u>oo</u> many <u>o's</u>.

stair and *stare*: I climb the st<u>air</u> in the <u>air</u>.

ROLL IT

Prepare a set of 20 word cards for each player. Choose words that match each child's grade level. Use sight words, words from the child's previous spelling lists, or grade-level words found online. Stack the cards in each set and place them facedown. The first player rolls a die and draws the matching number of cards from their stack of words. (If a 4 is rolled, they pick up 4 cards.) Have a helper read each word aloud as the player spells it. The player gets to keep the card for each word spelled correctly. For incorrect responses, the card goes back in the stack. Take turns rolling, drawing cards, and spelling. The first player with 10 cards is the winner.

WHAT TO DO WHEN YOUR CHILD STRUGGLES

As a parent, it is frustrating when your child has difficulties. When this happens, it is important to seek out help. Begin with your child's classroom teacher, who might be able to provide more personalized instruction and strategies to try at home. You can also reach out to a reading specialist or special education teacher at your school or district. Tutors, professionals in private practice, and reading clinics are other ways to support your child.

If your child continues to struggle, ask the school to have a meeting that includes the classroom teacher, reading or literacy coach, school psychologist, school counselor, and special education teacher. This is an opportunity for everyone to be honest and open in a supportive way. The goal of such a meeting is to gather information in order to decide how to move forward. Some possible outcomes are formal evaluation for special education, creation of a 504 Plan or Individualized Education Plan (IEP), more intensive instruction by the classroom teacher, or referral to a pediatrician for a possible medical diagnosis.

QUESTIONS FOR TEAM DISCUSSION

- Are there attention issues at school? At home?
- Is poor attendance having an impact?
- When were the child's hearing and vision last checked?
- Does the child speak another language?
- Did the child struggle with reading in previous grades?
- What supports and strategies have been in place? Were they successful?
- Does the child have a medical condition that may impact learning?

STUDY SKILLS

As your child begins getting more homework, they need to learn good study habits. These include organizing their backpack, breaking down assignments, and taking notes. Children who develop these skills in elementary school are more successful in middle school, high school, and beyond.

BACKPACK ORGANIZATION

An organized backpack saves time and helps your child be prepared. Set aside time every week to clean out and reorganize with your child.

1. Start with a clean and empty backpack.

2. Keep loose supplies in cases.

3. Assign a place for each item, and make sure everything gets returned to its spot.

4. Create a school-to-home folder for flyers and graded work. Have your child place items from this folder into a special bin at home and then immediately put the emptied folder back into the backpack.

5. Create a homework folder that is a different color than the school-to-home folder.

6. Use the agenda or planner that is provided or recommended by your child's school.

7. Ask for extra textbooks to keep at home if online versions are not available.

A PLACE TO STUDY

It is helpful to set up a place for your child to do homework, prepare for tests, and complete projects. Follow these guidelines.

- Pick a quiet, private place.
- Provide a good-sized desk or table and a comfortable chair.
- Make sure there is good lighting.
- Keep supplies close by.
- Provide shelves or bins for good storage and organization.

ESTABLISH ROUTINES

Routines help your child practice good habits. Checklists that you and your child create together are helpful reminders. Post them in easy-to-find areas around the house. Use this sample after-school checklist as a guide.

- ✔ Empty your school-to-home folder.
- ✔ Eat a snack.
- ✔ Do homework.
- ✔ Set the dinner table.
- ✔ Read for 30 minutes.
- ✔ Practice multiplication facts.

WORDS TO KNOW

504 Plan: a plan that describes the accommodations that the school will provide to support the student's education

active reading: when a reader is thinking about, involved with, and engaged in a text

decoding: the ability to sound out written words

ELA: English language arts

ELL: English language learner

ESE: exceptional student education

fluency: the ability to read with speed, accuracy, and appropriate expression

high-frequency word: a word that often appears in written material and that can be decoded using common phonics rules

IEP: individualized education plan; a personalized plan that describes the special education instruction, supports, and services a child needs

Lexile level: a scientific measurement of the complexity and readability of a text

literacy: the ability to read and write

phonemic awareness: the ability to identify and manipulate individual sounds in spoken words

phonics: matching the sounds of spoken English to individual letters or groups of letters; the relationship between sounds and letters

phonological awareness: the ability to identify and manipulate syllables and other parts of spoken words

reading comprehension: the ability to understand and interpret what you read

RTI: response to intervention; an educational strategy that aims to identify struggling students early on and give them the support they need to succeed in school

science of reading: a body of research that shows what is most important and effective in reading instruction

sight word: a word that often appears in written material and that can be difficult to decode using common phonics rules

standards: simple statements that describe what students are expected to know or do as a result of what is learned in school

syllable: a word part that contains one vowel sound

Tier 1 instruction: instruction for the whole class that is based on the learning standards for that grade level

Tier 2 instruction: small group instruction for students who demonstrate slight learning challenges in specific areas

Tier 3 instruction: small group instruction for students who need more intensive help and support

vocabulary: knowledge about what words mean

ADDITIONAL INFORMATION

To learn more about the science of reading:
https://teacherblog.evan-moor.com/2022/05/02/what-parents-need-to-know-about-the-science-of-reading/

To learn more about phonological awareness and phonemic awareness:
https://readingteacher.com/what-is-phonological-awareness-and-why-is-it-important/

To learn more about phonics and decoding:
https://www.twinkl.com/teaching-wiki/decoding

To learn more about vocabulary development:
https://www.edutopia.org/article/6-quick-strategies-build-vocabulary/

To learn more about reading comprehension:
https://www.readnaturally.com/research/5-components-of-reading/comprehension

To learn more about IEPs and 504 Plans:
https://www.understood.org/en/articles/the-difference-between-ieps-and-504-plans

Some information for this book came from the following websites:
- Florida Center for Reading Research https://fcrr.org
- Home Reading Helper https://www.homereadinghelper.org
- International Dyslexia Association https://dyslexiaida.org
- North Carolina Department of Public Instruction https://www.dpi.nc.gov
- Reading Rockets https://www.readingrockets.org

Written by: Madison Parker, M.Ed.
Design by: Rhea Magaro-Wallace
Series Development: James Earley
Editor: Kim Thompson

Photo credits: Shutterstock

Library of Congress PCN Data
Helping My Child with Reading Third Grade / Madison Parker, M.Ed.
A Guide to Supporting Reading
ISBN 979-8-89042-114-2 (paperback)
ISBN 979-8-89042-124-1 (eBook)
ISBN 979-8-89042-134-0 (ePUB)

Printed in the United States of America.

Seahorse Publishing Company

www.seahorsepub.com

Published in the United States
Seahorse Publishing
PO Box 771325
Coral Springs, FL 33077

Children whose parents are involved in schooling are more likely to have higher grades and test scores, to have better social skills, and to show improved behavior. This guide will help you understand the process of reading and how you can help your child build skills in comprehension, writing, vocabulary, and more.

SEAHORSE CONNECTIONS

SEAHORSE
PUBLISHING
seahorsepub.com

ISBN 979-8-8904-2114-2

90000

9 798890 421142